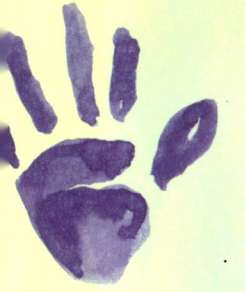

Psalm 139 for Kidz

"God knows all about me!"

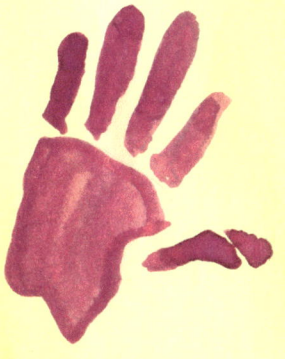

Lily,
Before your birth
God carefully planned
Who you would be!
Sherri T

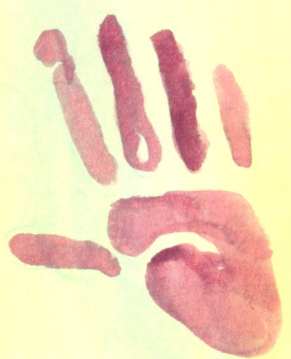

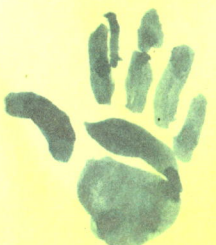

Author: Sherri Trudgian

Illustrator: Melanie Moreland

God knows
When I wake up —
Sees me hugging
My little pup.

God knows
What I will wear —
Out in the warm
Or chilly air.

God knows
All about me —
The things I do —
Who I will be.

God knows
What I will eat —
If it's healthy
Or something sweet.

God knows
Each thought, each word —
What I whisper
Before it's heard.

God knows
All about me —
The things I do —
Who I will be.

God sees me
Do my chores —
Or hide my junk
Behind the door.

God knows
All about me —
The things I do —
Who I will be.

God sees me
Try my best —
Or when I don't
And fail the test.

Sees me in
The corner chair —
Tears in my eyes,
Hugging my bear.

God knows
All about me —
The things I do —
Who I will be.

God sees me
Out with my friend —
Knows what's coming
Around the bend!

When I itch
With chicken pox —
He even knows
The number of   **SPOTS!**

God knows
All about me —
The things I do —
Who I will be.

Each moment
Sees where I am —
Sneaking cookies
Or blueberry jam!

God is there
Right by my side —
There's not a place
That I can hide.

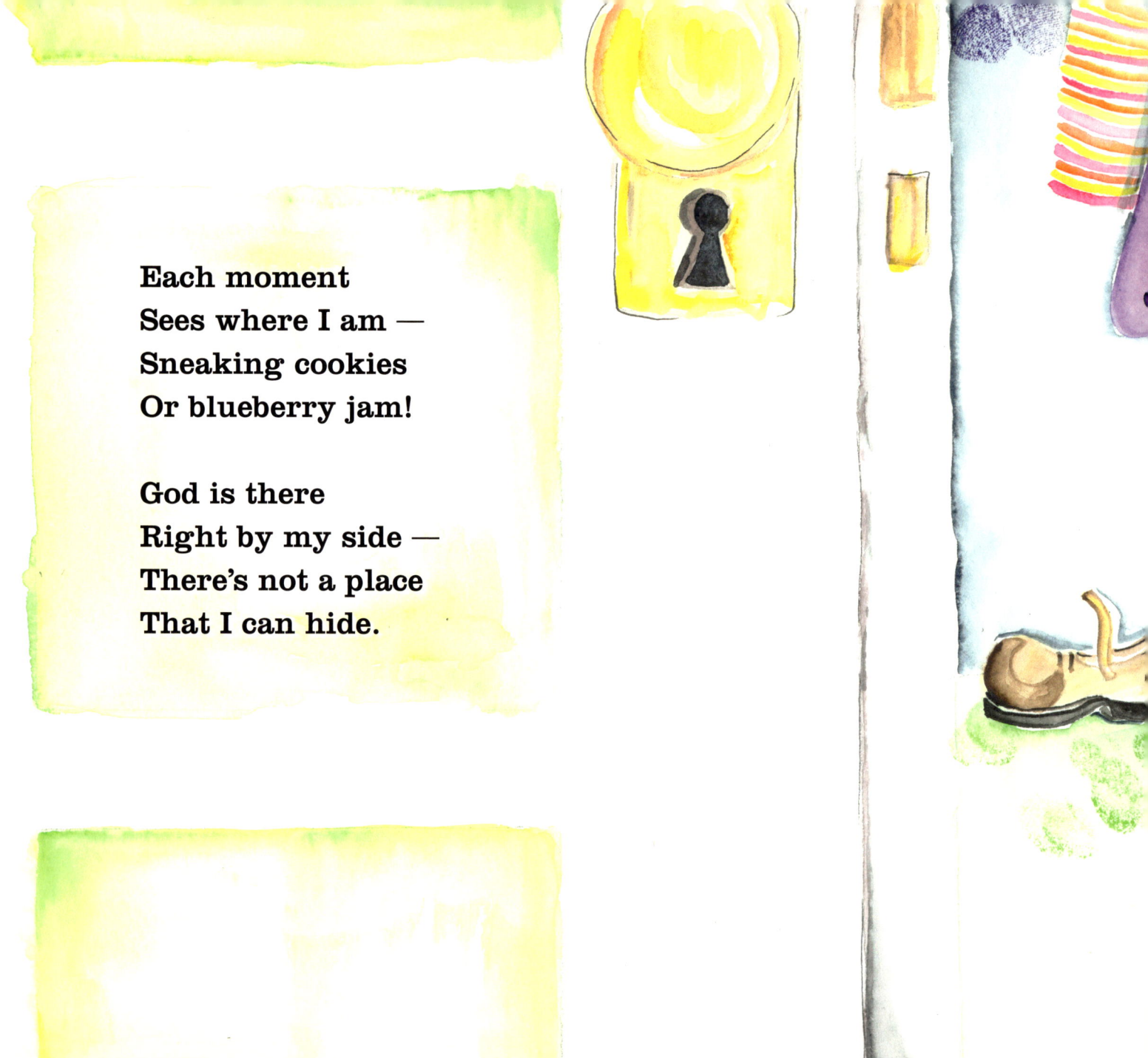

In my closet —
Under my bed —
With a pillow
Over my head!

The darkest dark
As it can be —
Is always light
To Him you see.

God knows
All about me —
The things I do —
Who I will be.

1 year

2 years

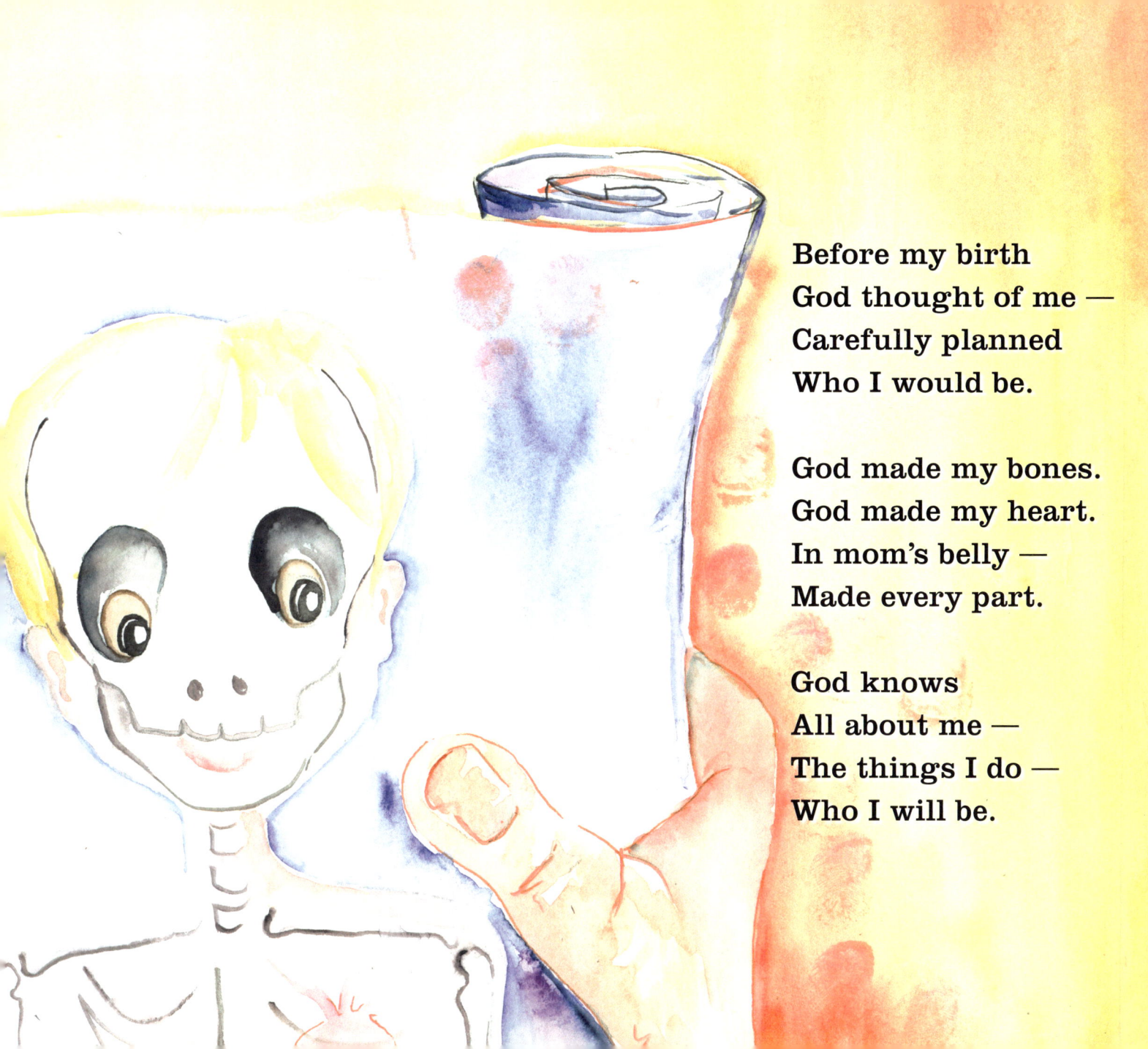

Before my birth
God thought of me —
Carefully planned
Who I would be.

God made my bones.
God made my heart.
In mom's belly —
Made every part.

God knows
All about me —
The things I do —
Who I will be.

God made my eyes.
He gave me two —
Some are dark brown,
Green or bright blue.

God picked the shape
Of my ears and nose —
Made ten fingers,
Ten wiggly toes.

God knows
All about me —
The things I do —
Who I will be.

Gave me muscles
So I could stretch —
Made joints and bones
To bend and catch.

He wrapped me up —
Colored my skin —
Made it stretch so
I could grow in.

Covered my skin
With tiny holes —
To sweat when hot —
Goosebumps when cold.

God knows
All about me —
The things I do —
Who I will be.

God picked the date
When I'd begin —
Chose the family
That I'd live in.

All of the parts
That come with me —
Fit together
Won-der-ful-ly!

I'm as happy
As I can be —
Thank you God for
Making me —   **ME!**

Psalm 139

(v. 1-7, 10-14)

O Lord … you know everything about me.

You know when I sit down or stand up.

You know my thoughts even when I'm far away.

You see me when I travel and when I rest at home.

You know everything I do.

You know what I am going to say

Even before I say it, Lord.

You go before me and follow me.

You place your hand of blessing on my head.

Such knowledge is too wonderful for me,

Too great for me to understand!

I can never escape from your Spirit!

I can never get away from your presence!

I could ask the darkness to hide me

And the light around me to become night —

But even in darkness I cannot hide from you.

To you the night shines as bright as day.

Darkness and light are the same to you.

You made all the delicate, inner parts of my body

And knit me together in my mother's womb.

Thank you for making me so wonderfully complex!

Your workmanship is marvelous — how well I know it.

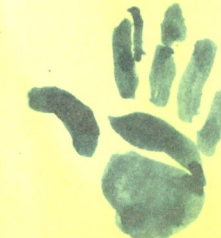